Cite as:
Fallucca, A., & Kniess, D. (2026). *Faculty and Staff Guide to Conducting Data Quality Evaluations.* National Resource Center for The First-Year Experience & Students in Transition, University of South Carolina. https://doi.org/10.65005/GRLE6459

ISBN: 978-1-942072-85-0 (paperback)
ISBN: 978-1-942072-86-7 (epub)

AF753811

Published by:
National Resource Center for The First-Year® Experience and Students in Transition
University of South Carolina
701 Assembly Street, Suite 1000, Columbia, SC 29201
www.sc.edu/fye

Production Staff for the National Resource Center:

Project Manager: Sean Cleary

Design and Production: Andrea Valaitis
Sean Cleary

Contents

About This Guide

Higher education data quality evaluations, synonymous with data audits, are becoming increasingly important to institutions aspiring to provide evidence of student learning and success to a variety of stakeholders. This evolution is spurred by increased accountability and the realization that decision-making requires insights gleaned through data, preferably collected over time and triangulated across multiple methods.

In essence, data audits emphasize a process of identifying data resources and associated uses within an institution with the goal of gathering them into a usable information system, such as a database or data repository (Paulson, 2003). It should be noted that significant data sources exist beyond student-focused areas; some examples include facilities dimensions, dining costs, and faculty metrics. Student data, including the significance of its disaggregation, is emphasized to support institutions conducting data quality evaluations with the priorities of student learning, transition, and success in mind.

A major rationale for engaging in data quality evaluations is that siloed thinking can lead to poorly informed and redundant, even contradictory data responses to organizational questions. As George Kuh (2016) noted, "Assessment is a device for change. Change moves at the speed of trust." Our aim is for conversations about data to begin with the foundational understanding that access and sharing of information benefits the organization's ability to thrive and adapt to a changing higher education landscape. These goals are dependent on the institution's ability to facilitate and advance data conversations that include a variety of recognized contributors.

The approaches provided here are developed for application within collaborative settings both internal and external to an organization (e.g., divisions or campuses), with a prevailing theme that data review processes should be mutually and extensively beneficial.

How to Use This Guide

This publication aims to serve program coordinators, department heads, data analysts, and institutional leadership across various institutional types and sizes. Individuals with varying levels of data expertise can also benefit, as the information is designed for cross-functional teams and extends beyond an individual role. A major goal of this guide is to provide resources and direction for facilitating data quality evaluations at readers' respective campuses or organizations. Another equally important aim is for institutions to build capacity for data collection, communication of results, and associated best practices, including the establishment of key partnerships to support current and future data-focused projects.

Glossary of Terms

Given this guide's purpose, a glossary of terms is established early to provide readers with a working vocabulary about data and aligned practices. This common language is also helpful when collaborating on a multi-partner and/or potentially complex project, as establishing familiar terms and definitions will help ensure key stakeholders are communicating information in similar ways. Additionally, language about data, assessment, research, and evaluation efforts can overlap or be misconstrued. The glossary helps ensure information communicated throughout this guide can support individuals within an organization, as they will be articulating key steps for successfully completing a data quality evaluation. As your organization advances through this process, feel free to add terms that will benefit the group and your overarching project.

! Key Terms

Accreditation: A process by which institutions or programs thoroughly review their data to demonstrate compliance with a set of standards established by an accrediting organization (Timm et al., 2013).

Analytics: An approach used in higher education to analyze various data points in order to gain insight and make informed decisions about complex issues. Specific areas include academic analytics, business intelligence, and learning analytics (EDUCAUSE, n.d.).

Assessment Cycle: A sequence of activities beginning with developing outcomes based on the mission and objectives of an institution, developing methods to collect the data, analyzing the data, then sharing results with internal and external stakeholders. From the previous cycle's results, new outcomes are created (Timm et al., 2013).

Assessment, Evaluation, Research (AER): The Assessment, Evaluation, and Research competency area is derived from the ACPA/NASPA Competencies (2015). The AER competency area centers on the ability to design, conduct, critique, and use various methodologies and the results obtained from them to utilize AER processes and their results to inform practice, as well as shape the political and ethical climate surrounding AER processes and uses in higher education (p. 13).

Audit: An official inspection of the department or institution's data or accounts by an independent body.

Benchmarking: Comparative, normative, or norm-referenced benchmarks internal or external to an organization (Suskie, 2009, p. 236). For example, institutions might keep a list of peer institutions and aspirant institutions to compare how their institution scores on a specific measure.

Dashboards: Visual representations of data intended to give the "30,000-foot view of an organization's key performance indicators," typically on a single page for department directors and administrative leaders (Evergreen, 2018, p. 15).

Data Ethics: A code of behavior that describes appropriate ways of handling data (Knight, 2021).

Data Steward: The individual responsible for the management and proficiency of data stored within an organization. A data steward knows how data are collected, maintained, and interpreted at the organization (Hebbar, 2017).

Demographics: Statistical data relating to the population and particular groups within it.

Direct Measures: Tangible and compelling evidence that demonstrates student learning, such as objective exams, evaluations of demonstrations, and portfolios (Timm et al., 2013).

Formative Measures: Data gathered in the process of a program, process, or learning experience that can be used to make changes as the program or experience progresses (Timm et al., 2013).

Indirect Measures: Data gathered from questionnaires and interviews asking students or others to reflect on their learning rather than demonstrate it (Banta & Palomba, 2015, p. 23).

Institutional Readiness: Level of interest, enthusiasm, or capacity of higher education organizations to infuse information technology into new or existing processes (adapted from Twigg, 2000).

IRB (Institutional Review Board): A group of individuals at an institution with the responsibility of ensuring the ethical and responsible conduct of research using human subjects.

Key Performance Indicators (KPIs): Quantitative measures of overall student or organizational performance (Suskie, 2009, p. 117).

Learning Outcomes: Goals established at the beginning of a program or experience that indicate "the knowledge, skills, attitudes, and habits of mind that students take with them from a learning experience" (Suskie, 2009, p. 117).

Population: All the individuals of interest who are being studied.

Representativeness: A subset of a population that seeks to accurately represent the larger group.

Response Rate: The number of individuals who answered a survey or questionnaire divided by the total number of people in the sample.

Rubric: A scoring tool that establishes specific criteria for performance in which information is evaluated (Stevens & Levi, 2013, p. 3).

Sample: A set of individuals selected from a population, typically intended to represent the population in a research study.

Summative Measures: Data collection at the end of a program, process, or learning experience to make judgements about quality compared to previously designed standards for performance (Banta & Palomba, 2015, p. 19).

Validity: An instrument's ability to measure what it is intended to measure, which includes construct, criterion, and content validity (Timm et al., 2013).

Variables: A characteristic or condition that changes or has different values for different individuals.

**Add additional terms to the list specific to your project and campus needs:*

Term	Agreed-upon definition based on literature, best practices, and localized utility

Putting Concepts Into Practice

This guide provides recommended activities to advance readers' understanding and application of successful data quality evaluation strategies. To illustrate these points and showcase a rationale to organizational stakeholders about the need for such exercises, we provide an example case study **(see Appendix A)** for you to consider and analyze.

Why Conduct a Data Quality Evaluation?

In the past decade, the higher education landscape has shifted dramatically in terms of the diversity of students attending colleges and universities nationwide. Lower numbers of traditional college-age students (18-year-olds) graduating from high school, combined with the rising cost of college tuition, caused more individuals to question the value of a degree (Delaney & Marcotte, 2023; Looney, 2024). In addition, enrollment for traditional-age college students is expected to decline in 2026 (Grawe, 2017), and impacts of the Covid-19 pandemic continue to influence admission processes at two- and four-year institutions (Kamssu & Kouam, 2021). Consequently, institutions face increasing challenges in retaining and graduating current students.

When analyzing both the higher education enrollment results and retention metrics, particularly for marginalized and underserved populations, it is imperative to leverage data to understand which student populations are retained through graduation. Data quality evaluations help identify institutional data gaps that can create unintended barriers and limit what is known about students and their experiences. As such, the ability to identify trustworthy data sources that speak to students' developing knowledge and overarching college experiences is essential to describing their progress.

Significant reasons to evaluate data quality exist beyond institutional decision-making, including responding to regional accreditation and similar accountability standards at the program, institutional, and state levels. Further, data quality evaluations help to establish positive culture around data utilization, which in turn helps increase trust among stakeholders and the likelihood of effectively employing existing data, as opposed to investing resources into something additive and singularly useful. This validation of data also centers on the principle that institutional constituents, especially students, deserve useful, quality information to make informed decisions that impact their coursework selection, involvement in co-curricular experiences, and allocation of time (Swing & Ross, 2016).

Several significant publications relating to institutional processes and best practices for student data exist, including those in support of underrepresented populations (University of Southern California Center for Urban Education, n.d.), community college students (Achieving the Dream, n.d.), and students raising families (American Talent Initiative, n.d.). In collaboration with the Policy Center on the First Year of College (now known as the John N. Gardner Institute for Excellence in Higher Education) and the National Center for Higher Education Management Systems (NCHEMS), Karen Paulson (2003) published a data audit and analysis toolkit specific to first-year college assessment practices. This important contribution highlighted the need for institutions to capture student-level data, thus moving away from the more traditional aggregate analyses methods. It also emphasized thinking about data as a collection of key indicators to inform our understanding of student experiences; as such, disparate and siloed data sources are less effective.

More than 20 years later, a data science revolution and its critical inclusion in higher education assessment is clearly visible. While data sources and technology platforms might have increased substantially over time, the method by which campuses connect information on a consistent basis, particularly student-level data, is far less developed. This publication addresses some of the prevailing challenges in continuing to move the needle on data audit best practices.

Data Quality Evaluation Conceptual Framework

We introduce the Readiness, Examination, and Interpretation (REI) conceptual framework, emphasizing three key components to support a comprehensive approach to data quality evaluations (Figure 1). The data quality evaluation framework is associated with Astin's Input-Environment-Output (IEO) Model (1970b; 1991), with a visible emphasis on entry, environmental, and outcome stages.

Our model describes Readiness as the alignment of organizational readiness factors to successfully participate in data audits. The Examination stage speaks to the ability to access various data sources, at the institution as well as state, system, consortium, and national levels. The Interpretation stage represents the interpretation of findings and action steps that will develop because of this data review process. The structure can help data advocates categorize evidence-based sources and related data steward roles such that even complex organizations can benefit from its utility and application.

Figure 1.
Visual Representation of REI Conceptual Framework

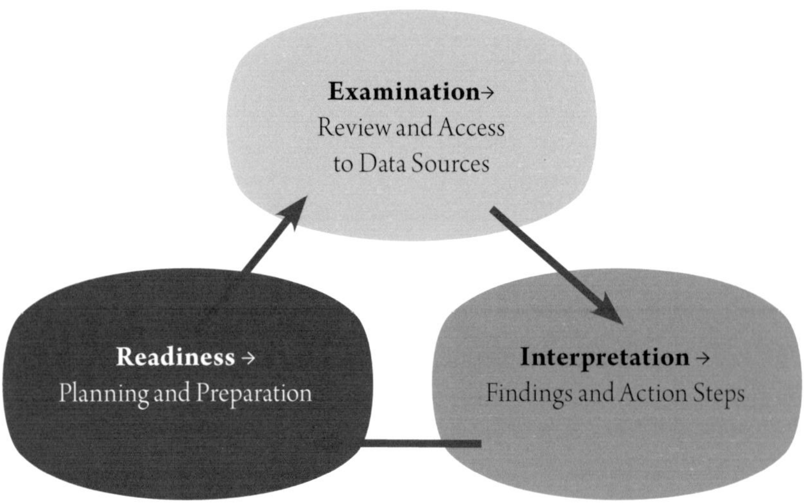

Readiness: Planning and Preparation Stages

In higher education, sustained motivation and interest across initiatives typically develop from an identified need, significant request, or visible opportunity. Given this premise, ask yourself and your team the following questions:

1. What will be the driving forces for initiating the data quality evaluation?

2. After making this data review decision, what expectations and other considerations are in place to help set the organization up for success?

Discussions on these topics are encouraged before initiating the action steps aligned with completing this data review process. While every timeline might be different, we recommend beginning these conversations 1-3 months before taking formal actions, starting with a data audit.

The following key actions should be addressed before the data quality evaluation and updated throughout its implementation. Responses will vary by the institution, project scope, and individuals contributing to the overall process. It is also important to continually revisit these steps throughout the audit to ensure the team and accompanying actions stay on track and that all members are apprised of the overarching goals.

Five Data Quality Evaluation Actions:

1. Establish the purpose of the data quality evaluation.
    - Why is the data review process being facilitated, and what are the intentions of this exercise?
2. Identify objectives to inform project performance.
    - What are we trying to achieve through this data review process?
    - Can we state the key components that will inform our action steps?
3. Craft a problem statement that reflects the purpose and objectives.
    - Can the purpose and objectives be written as a concise description of the problem that needs to be solved?
4. Create a reasonable timeline for the data quality evaluation, including start date, major milestones, and end date.
    - What key benchmarks and deadlines will inform the data review progress?
    - When should we expect the data review to be completed?
5. Define success criteria for the process.
    - Based upon the purpose, objectives, and timeline, how will success be defined?
    - How will progress be measured and made evident to constituents?

Data Readiness Checklist

Following preparation steps will support your successful implementation of the data quality evaluation. The following checklist activity involves key stakeholders and describes one method of understanding institutional readiness. This exercise can be completed independently and then communicated within a larger group, as the unique member perspectives can expose previously unfamiliar or unknown opinions. A subsequent collaborative conversation about the checklist will not only help determine overall preparations, but also likely elicit new ideas or strategies beyond the immediate data quality evaluation process.

Faculty and Staff Guide to Conducting Data Quality Evaluations (Fallucca & Kniess, 2026)

Data Quality Evaluation Checklist

Introduction: The ideal conditions for a promising data quality evaluation require an overarching institutional commitment to the process, particularly when unexpected or surprising results develop that could potentially place your program or campus in a negative light. Directed conversations should involve questions such as:

- *What is our current readiness to engage in this data review process?*
- *Have we established appropriate buy-in from key stakeholders* (participants as well as those in influential leadership support roles)?
- *Would another initiative or institutional focus* (e.g., strategic plan, accreditation process) *potentially benefit from, or factor into, the data audit process?*

Engaging in these conversations early in the process is important, as they will help set the foundation for a successful progression and use of data quality evaluation findings once the formal actions are complete.

Checklist: Use this to explore and gain understanding of your institution's current readiness toward engaging in a data quality evaluation.	
1. What artifacts or symbols exist that demonstrate an organizational commitment to data?	*Name as many as you can think of:*
2. Does your organization exhibit the following actions?	*Write Yes or No (Y/N) for the following statements. If yes, please give an example:*

a. Committee structures are focused on data collection and usage. b. Data/assessment "champions" are members of collaborative projects or committees. c. There is an expectation of data updates and discussions related to results as part of unit or program meeting agendas. d. Data commitments and actions are included in job descriptions (as a percentage of the role). e. Technology support and access is visible (e.g., via analysis and assessment software). f. Related websites or newsletters are shared across the organization. g. Data is accessible through appropriate channels with reasonable trust about its utilization.	

3. Are data and assessment recognized or celebrated within the organization?	*Write Yes or No (Y/N) for the following statements. If yes, please give an example:*
a. Events dedicated to sharing of results are visible (e.g.), poster presentations). b. Professional development opportunities are afforded in areas related to data (e.g., trainings, conferences, shared publications). c. Influential leaders regularly request data to use as part of decision-making processes and state the data's value to internal audiences and external stakeholders.	

4. Who owns access *or* controls access to your data (e.g., open access, a specific department/ unit, academic division, data analytics officer, enrollment management office, technology vendor, senior level administrators)?	*Identify connections between who oversees data within different departments or units at the institution and how that could impact data sharing and cross-functional assessment practices.*

Reflection:

After completing the checklist, I realized/I observed/ I learned/I gained, etc. ...

After completing the checklist, I will ________________________ ____________________________ to increase individual or institutional readiness. *(Name one action step you can take as a result of completing this checklist.)*

Engaging in the data quality evaluation checklist, including sharing its key findings, can help shape institutional culture around data and assessment activities as well as cross-campus collaboration. It is also useful to think about this tool as a means of tracking progress over time for cultivating a positive assessment culture (Henning & Roberts, 2016). A visible commitment to data activities such as these will help demonstrate institutional support for the value of data among a variety of stakeholders. Note that the checklist is not exhaustive, and the process could require more steps than originally intended (e.g., questions might need to be added or revisited).

Time and Resources

Once readiness levels are addressed with a commitment to advance the data quality evaluation process, it is important to determine a timeline, including the procedural actions and subsequent decisions impacting future changes within the organization. For example, does a summer period or other traditionally designated "down time" make sense given the project parameters? Or is there an existing annual report or planning cycle that can inform when the data audit is completed? Is there momentum and a need for such a process with respect to accreditation, self-study, program certification, and/or strategic planning processes?

Pros and cons exist in establishing a data quality evaluation in tandem with current data cycles, given the resources and personnel involved. For example, if individuals within a student affairs division are expected to complete an annual report outlining both internal-level (e.g., unit, initiative) and related external-level data (e.g., campus partner, national), should the same roles support a parallel data quality evaluation? A benefit is that individuals closest to a traditional data process with an understanding of the depth of institutional sources are involved. Conversely, using staff more external to routine data activities could allow for a more authentic critique of current processes.

Specific to resources, both acknowledged institutional support and a recognition of how individuals leading the audit will be supported during the process is essential. Examples of resource commitments could include: meeting space, access to technology or institutional information, support for the creation or development of materials, potential compensation or release time from obligations, or even recognition. Outlining resource needs and availability before beginning the data quality evaluation actions will help set expectations and demonstrate commitment to the evaluation's overall value.

Key Stakeholders

Depending on the scope of the data quality evaluations, it might be beneficial to establish a committee or working group focused on a particular data goal to address institutional data questions through recommendations. This group does not need to be extensively large; in fact, smaller groups will likely help ensure timely completion while also easing communication. It is also possible to establish formal roles, with those on the periphery participating at specific times in the process. A formal draft of the project purpose and expectations for participants should be available to committee members, and their feedback should be incorporated before finalizing the charge.

For this group, representation across campus constituents helps to encourage a collaborative space while also acknowledging unique perspectives that can contribute to the overarching data quality evaluation goals. Depending on the project's scope, group membership could include representatives in the following table. Consider who from your institution could best serve in this role.

Table 1: *Potential Key Stakeholders for Addressing Institutional Data Questions (Larger Institutions)*	
Suggested representative area	**Potential member(s) from institution**
Academic Affairs (administrative role/user)	
Business Affairs/Finance	
Faculty (typically those invested in the data)	
Individual unit or program (could be "frontline" data creators and consumers, as well as leadership roles)	
Institutional Research	
Information Technology	
Registrar's Office/Enrollment Management	
Student Affairs, including academic and staff advisors	

Additional functional areas specific to your institutional profile, or those familiar with existing data efforts or holding related data expertise	

For smaller institutions, or where less complex administrative structures exist, a 3-4 person team could be effective. Consider identifying a key data steward, a frontline consumer/user, and a more senior leader to participate.

Table 2: *Potential Key Stakeholders for Addressing Institutional Data Questions (Smaller Institutions)*

Suggested membership	**Potential members from institution**
Key data steward (institutional research or information technology)	
Frontline consumer/user (frequent requester and user of institutional data situated within a department or unit)	
Senior leader role (high-level view and understanding of priority projects in which data is an asset for decision-making)	

Support for Completion/Commitment to Actions

Before fully engaging in the data quality evaluation process, discuss with key leaders how your project findings will inform next steps. At times, data collection and analysis efforts are viewed as a completion of the process, as opposed to a vehicle leading to additional review and subsequent actions. This step toward "closing the loop" helps to validate efforts and also highlights the rationale for original data inquiries. Given that these steps might be somewhat nebulous at this point in the project planning, the group will at minimum need reassurance that the data quality evaluation findings will be reviewed and shared, and that actions will be considered based on their recommendations. This commitment extends to all gleaned insights, including those that will require additional steps to successfully meet data project expectations moving forward.

It is possible that some anticipated outcomes exist in the process or can be loosely identified (e.g., a deficit of student-level information related to career placement of graduates by college or specific years that needs to be addressed). When possible, these outcomes should be identified in advance and clearly presented as part of the overall project planning process.

Examination: Review and Access to Data Sources

As your team or division undertakes this data review, consider the types of information the institution collects and where the data is housed within the institution. Several areas within student affairs (including student groups), academic affairs, and business operations collect data on student retention, use of campus services, career placement of graduates, and even budget efficiencies. For example, your campus might have a history of using institution-based systems (e.g., Anthology, Tableau) as a repository for survey or national data that you could access with permission. National-level resources also exist, such as College Navigator and the Integrated Postsecondary Education Data System (IPEDS), both of which contain information on the performance and persistence of student cohorts. If your institution traditionally participates in national surveys such as the National Survey for Student Engagement (NSSE), the CIRP Freshman Survey, Education Advisory Board (EAB) campus climate, or Noel Levitz surveys, this data can also be part of your data quality evaluation.

Data Quality Evaluation Activity

To help identify existing sources, team members are encouraged to complete the following data review activity individually and then share across the group to see where similar and different findings emerge. This kind of "self-evaluation" can help understand where saturation (i.e., a point where gathering data reveals no new information) or likely sources exist, while also acknowledging data that was overlooked as a resource or is missing altogether. Team members are encouraged to discuss the findings and meaning behind the responses and how the outcomes inform data quality evaluation steps moving forward, particularly relating to ideas, reflections, or epiphanies they had during this exercise (see Question 9, below).

1a. Take one minute to list as many potential sources of data on students and student experiences on your campus as possible (making a T column is recommended; see Question 1b):

Potential Sources of Data on Students and Student Experiences	Responsible Party

1b. Go back through your list above and write the name of a responsible party (list the individual or office) next to as many of the "Potential Sources of Data" items as possible.

2. Each of the following areas represents a potential source of data. Please indicate whether your campus has this data source, doesn't have it, or if you I don't know or can't find out. Note that these data sources could house information from a number of engagement types, including (examples in parentheses): transactional (meal swipes), usage (website visits), satisfaction (survey), learning (assignment evaluation), development (alumni donations), or sales (bookstore). This is NOT a comprehensive list. Please feel free to add to it.

Data Source:	Yes	No	I Don't Know	Notes (where do the data reside, who is in charge of it, how is it used, do you need it, etc.)
Academic Services				
Academic awards and honors				
Academic records/grades				
Academic support office use				
Accreditation				
Admissions				
Advising utilization & records				
Athletics/sports information				

Data Source:	Yes	No	I Don't Know	Notes (where do the data reside, who is in charge of it, how is it used, do you need it, etc.)
Bookstore usage/sales data				
Campus activities				
Campus ministry				
Career placement				
Career services				
Classroom utilization & satisfaction				
Communications to faculty				
Communications to public (PR)				
Communications to staff				
Communications to students				

Data Source:	Yes	No	I Don't Know	Notes (where do the data reside, who is in charge of it, how is it used, do you need it, etc.)
Communications to students' families				
Community engagement				
Cooperative Institutional Research Program (CIRP)				
Counseling services				
Course evaluations				
Course information				
Course syllabi				
Course textbooks and materials				
Cultural event participation				
Cultural organization engagement				

Data Source:	Yes	No	I Don't Know	Notes (where do the data reside, who is in charge of it, how is it used, do you need it, etc.)
Developmental education information/reports				
Dining services				
Disability services/ information				
Emergency aid				
Facilities usage and satisfaction				
Faculty/personnel information				
Field placements				
Financial aid awards & information				
Fitness center engagement				
Greek life				
Housing				

Data Source:	Yes	No	I Don't Know	Notes (where do the data reside, who is in charge of it, how is it used, do you need it, etc.)
Information technology services use/engagement				
Institutional research data & reports				
Internships/co-ops				
IPEDs data				
Judicial affairs				
Laboratory utilization & satisfaction				
Learning Center/ Student Success Center use				
Legal services for students				
LGBTQ+ services				
Library usage/ engagement				

Data Source:	Yes	No	I Don't Know	Notes (where do the data reside, who is in charge of it, how is it used, do you need it, etc.)
National Survey of Student Engagement				
Orientation services				
Peer leadership opportunities				
Placement testing and data				
Prerequisite information				
Registration				
Schedule of classes				
Scholarships/grants				
Service learning				
Student employment				
Student information systems				

Data Source:	Yes	No	I Don't Know	Notes (where do the data reside, who is in charge of it, how is it used, do you need it, etc.)
Student life data				
Student surveys: Homegrown				
Student surveys: National tools				
Study abroad				
Supplemental instruction				
Tutoring				
Wellness & health services				
Women's career services				
Other:				
Other:				
Other:				

3. Please go through and highlight the 10 most commonly used data sources at your institution.

4. Please go through and star up to five data sources that you regularly access or use as part of your efforts.

5. Please list five sources of data you do not currently have or do not currently use that you see as critical to establishing a coordinated approach to student success:

6. Please list at least three sources of data for which you marked "I Don't Know." What strategies will help you find out whether your institution has that information?

7. Based on your data quality evaluation, who are three critical partners for data access, utilization, and analysis?

8. What ideas do you have for approaching the three critical partners listed above about advancing your data collaboration?

9. Please capture any other ideas, reflections, or epiphanies you had during this exercise:

(Activity adapted from "Campus Integration Analysis Professional Learning Communities" as developed by the National Resource Center for The First-Year Experience and Students in Transition.)

By design, this data review activity represents a combination of reflective and action-oriented steps leading to significant takeaways and suggested implementation goals. Refer back to the Five Data Quality Evaluation Actions on page 12 to revisit the intended purpose and objectives. Documenting respective individual responses to the activity can help maintain momentum moving forward; this information can also help determine whether someone on your team might have expertise or a key contact in the specific area to assign tasks.

Be sure to leave time for any remaining data-cleaning procedures, including streamlining datasets or even combining them when needed. These steps could either be assigned within the committee structure, or as part of the resource request for additional data analyst expertise. Once these steps are completed, the team can leverage members' diverse perspectives to help inform interpretation of the collected data points. These conversations are beneficial, as varied institutional perspectives can lead to future collaborations and data-driven decision-making.

Another important consideration involves how data are communicated. As your team determines what data are available and how to access it, determining whether and how your team manipulates the data is key. Key Performance Indicators (KPIs), dashboards, and executive summaries are all useful ways to communicate data to specific audiences.

> Schuh et al. (2016) described Clemson University's use of a one-page "Student Affairs Dashboard," with a gear shift and the symbols of "D" (drive), "N" (neutral), or "R" (reverse) to report progress in six student affairs goal areas (p. 306). A narrative for each of the six goals was provided in addition to a description of next steps to highlight areas of opportunity in retention, student engagement, and organizational efficiencies. **(see Appendix B)**

Interpretation: Findings and Action Steps

Congratulations! This is an exciting stage for data quality evaluation champions. Your efforts will likely produce promising practices for implementation, but also actions that will improve overall decision-making and sharing of data across your organization. Maintaining this momentum as you consider key next steps is important. In case you are not feeling as confident as you would like or still have outstanding questions, from a positive standpoint, data quality evaluation processes are iterative in nature. Therefore, the REI Conceptual Framework can be distilled and revisited to see where additional energies can be spent.

Analysis of Data Quality Evaluation and Development of Procedures

Upon completion, it will be important to revisit the original impetus for the data quality evaluation and the agreed-upon responses to the Five Data Quality Evaluation Actions (see page 7). A variety of insights could emerge through the data review process, and those will be key in determining the best route forward for your institution. Examples include developing locally recognized sources for student data, accessible databases or platforms providing timely responses or output to institutional questions, and longitudinally developed and trusted datasets. These takeaways will help affirm current practices and personnel actions.

Some additional potential findings could include:

- Data are deficient overall, suggesting they are not being collected in ways that could inform priority institutional questions.
- Data are being collected but not used effectively. Potential reasons for this include:
    - Data lack organization . The data are not uniformly located or made visible in a way that is easily understood or manipulated.

- Data are not "good." The data lack validity because of poor definition or standardization.
- Data are irrelevant. The data do not align well with current needs or objectives. If deemed arbitrary in nature, data can be edited or removed. If deemed not usable, it is appropriate practice to stop collecting data. If they are deemed helpful later, there might be an opportunity to restart data collection.
- Data are not being shared or used as part of decision-making processes. Data are fallible to non-use if steps toward "closing the loop" are not completed. An institutional commitment is needed to help ensure these actions; supportive buy-in and cultures can be helpful in this process.

- Additional takeaways could focus on a commitment to revisiting the identification and communication of campus data definitions (e.g., defining "resident" or "college GPA" so readers can interpret data being shared). A designated responsibility within a committee structure could entail managing the repository, as well as gathering new terms and defining them according to specific campus language.
- Furthermore, a result of data quality evaluations could elevate the significance of shared governance structures within campuses or organizations. A committee of participants could develop policies and procedures, yielding greater access to data and how units will request and use this information. This committee could be situated within information technology departments, or as a joint venture with institutional research and assessment offices (Wisconsin Technical College System, 2019). Consideration should be given to how data audit participants can contribute, so that future planning efforts can be bridged with historical actions.

Communication of Data Quality Evaluation Findings

As part of the process of closing the loop, it is important to identify methods for communicating the data project findings. Sharing insights from the data quality evaluation can increase transparency and overall buy-in. Some recommended actions include:

- **A formal summary:** Written documentation is key to tracking the process of planning and implementing the data audit. It will be important to synthesize the key points through a shareable summary that can be oriented to a variety of campus audiences.
- **An open forum:** One consideration for sharing key updates, findings, and recommendations is through an organized presentation by the data audit committee, with opportunities for questions and dialogue. This session could be implemented at an ending point but could also be beneficial if regular updates

are shared along the way. Depending on the size and scope of the data review process, this event could be smaller or larger in nature as deemed appropriate.

- **Regular communications updates:** A commitment to communicating information past the initial data quality evaluation could take the form of regular newsletters or community listservs. Communication could focus on project updates, sharing of results, and professional development opportunities (e.g., accessing and learning new assessment-based software).

Commitment to Resources to Support Data Culture and Implementation Stages

Concluding this data review process will also bring forward suggested action steps related to resource allotment and data culture development goals. Some ways these goals can be realized include:

- **Establishing a values statement about data and who is intended to benefit from the institutional commitment to its utility:** Including student perspectives will help ensure their college experiences are prioritized. Astin et al. (1993) provide a resource for beginning these assessment values discussions.
- **Revisiting current staffing structures and personnel dedicated to data collection and management:** If deemed appropriate, can current position descriptions be revised or new roles created?
- **Establishing systematic support through software, platforms, and databases:** Is your institution committed to providing quality, efficient tools to support your personnel with data management?
- **For all stakeholders, a commitment to trainings and professional development:** How will the institution ensure it is on the cutting edge of understanding best practices and trends in the field across various data users?
- **Creating dedicated spaces for having candid conversations about data:** This step includes stated methods for requesting, accessing, interpreting, and sharing data project-related processes (e.g., new and innovative analyses and findings).

Frequency of Data Quality Evaluations

Going forward, discussing the frequency of data reviews within your organization will be important. Many factors will contribute to this institutional decision, as individual campuses might approach timing in different ways. For example, determining the time and resources required to address identified gaps will influence a potential next future cycle of review. Significant staff turnover could also impact the likelihood of or the need to revisit a data audit exercise to help ensure key stakeholders know about the status of data needs and sources. As future data processes come into focus, revisiting the Five Data Quality Evaluation Actions will help ensure successful preparations and clarity of actions.

Realistic Approach

Evaluating the overall process at the conclusion of the data quality evaluations will be key. What does this data review not accomplish—and therefore, what additional recommended sources or actions should be taken? For example, if findings show visible data gaps across units, how will the organization look to extend itself beyond the data audit to ensure such differences are addressed? Further, what stumbling blocks or inefficiencies emerged during the data audit process? These steps can be reevaluated with identified action plans for improvement moving forward. A potential solution could involve a committee structure dedicated to the identification and ethical use of data, as well as the establishment of a data repository or system to help overcome potential future challenges. The new system should be regularly evaluated for its responsiveness to institutional data questions.

Recommended Literature/Best Practices

Questions and identified topical gaps related to the data quality evaluation exercise will likely emerge. One recommended approach is to review current best practices and relevant literature. Consider completing additional outreach to institutions or organizations that have made promising strides.

A variety of scholarly sources can also help guide collective thinking. Sharing this information helps educate stakeholders on what data reviews are intended to do, as well as helping establish a common language and understanding for realistic expectations within your own organization. Some examples follow:

*

Higher Education Data Resources

Periodicals:

- *Assessment Update*
- *Journal of Educational Data Mining*
- *Journal of Learning Analytics*
- *Research & Practice in Assessment*

Online resources:

- American Institutes for Research (AIR): https://www.air.org/
- Consortium for Student Retention Data Exchange (CSRDE): https://csrde.ou.edu/
- Higher Education Data Sharing Consortium: https://www.hedsconsortium.org/
- Integrated Postsecondary Education Data System: https://nces.ed.gov/ipeds/ and College Navigator: https://nces.ed.gov/collegenavigator/

Be sure to continue adding to your own campus library of resources!

Conclusion

Data collection and its utilization in decision-making is a necessary practice that will guide higher education and its inevitable evolution moving forward. The institutions that prepare for such adaptations will undoubtedly persevere, and likely thrive, in part because of dedicated and consistent data planning. Data quality evaluations serve as a means of advancing positive assessment-based culture, while providing strategies to better understand localized and external sources and apply them to critical institutional questions. This guide is intended to support individual and collective thinking about the value proposition of data at higher education institutions. Our hope is that, with these recommended tools and strategies in hand, institutions can continue this exciting process. Consider this a call to action to advance your data interests!

References

Achieving the Dream. (n.d.). *Data and technology assessment.* www.achievingthedream.org/services-supports/data-and-technology-assessment

ACPA: College Student Educators International & NASPA: Student Affairs Administrators in Higher Education (2015). *ACPA/NASPA professional competency areas for student affairs practitioners.* Authors.

American Talent Initiative. (n.d.). *Progress.* https://americantalentinitiative.org/progress/

Astin, A. W. (1970b). The methodology of research on college impact. *Sociology of Education, 43,* 223–254.

Astin, A. W. (1991). *Assessment for excellence: The philosophy and practice of assessment and evaluation in higher education.* McMillan.

Astin, A. W., Banta, T. W., Cross, P., El-Khawas, E., Ewell, P. T., Hutchings, P., Marchese, T. J., McClenney, K. M., Mentkowski, M., Miller, M. A., Moran, E. T., & Wright, B. D. (1993). Nine principles of good practice for assessing student learning. *Leadership Abstracts, 6(4).*

Banta, T. W., & Palomba, C. A. (2015). *Assessment essentials: Planning, implementing, and improving assessment in higher education.* Jossey-Bass. Counting Opinions. (n.d.). Assessment quotes. Counting Opinions. Retrieved September 2, 2025, from https://www.countingopinions.com

Delaney, T., & Marcotte, D. E. (2023). The cost of public higher education and college enrollment. *The Journal of Higher Education, 95(4),* 496–525.

EDUCAUSE. (n.d.) *Analytics* [Webpage]. www.educause.edu/focus-areas-and-initiatives/enterprise-and-infrastructure/enterprise-it-program/analytics

Evergreen, S. (2018). *Presenting data effectively: Communicating your findings for maximum impact (2nd ed.).* Sage Publications.

Grawe, N. (2017). *Demographics and the demand for higher education.* Johns Hopkins University Press.

Hebbar, P. (2017, Sept. 26). What is data steward and what are their roles and responsibilities? *Analytics India Magazine.* https://analyticsindiamag.com/data-steward-roles-responsibilities

Henning, G. W., & Roberts, D. M. (2016). *Student affairs assessment: Theory to practice.* Routledge.

Kamssu, A. J., & Kouam, R. B. (2021). The effects of the COVID-19 pandemic on university student enrollment decisions and higher education resource allocation. *Journal of Higher Education Theory and Practice, 21(12),* 143–153.

Knight, M. (2021, May 19). *What is data ethics?* Dataversity. www.dataversity.net/what-are-data-ethics/

Kuh, G. (2016, October 16). *Past as prologue: Advancing the assessment agenda by avoiding pitfalls of our own making* [Conference session]. Assessment Institute, Indianapolis, IN, United States.

Looney, A. (2024). How much does college cost and how does it relate to student borrowing? Tuition growth and borrowing over the past 30 years. *National Tax Journal, 77(3),* 605–622.

Paulson, K. (2003). *A data audit and analysis toolkit to support assessment of the first college year, administrative rationale and technical manual.* Policy Center on the First Year of College and the National Center for Higher Education Management Systems.

Schuh, J. N., Biddix, J. P., Dean, L. A., & Kinzie, J. (2016). *Assessment in student affairs (2nd ed.).* Jossey-Bass.

Stevens, D. D., & Levi, A. J. (2013). *Introduction to rubrics (2nd ed.).* Stylus.

Suskie, L. (2009). *Assessing student learning: A common sense guide (2nd ed.).* Jossey-Bass.

Swing, R. L., and Ross, L. E. (2016). *Statement of Aspirational Practice for Institutional Research.* Association for Institutional Research. Retrieved January 8, 2025 from www.airweb.org/aspirationalstatement.

Timm, D. M., Davis Barham. J., McKinney, J., & Knerr, A. R. (2013). *Assessment in practice: A companion guide to the ASK standards.* ACPA-College Student Educators International.

Twigg, C. (2000). Institutional readiness criteria. *Educause Review, 35(2),* 42–48, 50–51.

University of Southern California Center for Urban Education. (n.d.) *Equity Scorecard* [Webpage]. https://cue.usc.edu/tools/the-equity-scorecard/

Wisconsin Technical College System. (2019). *Data governance toolkit.* https://pdfcoffee.com/data-governance-toolkit-pdf-free.html

Appendix A

Case Study: XYZ University

An alumnus from XYZ University has approached the vice president of university advancement to inquire about donating a $100,000 recurring gift to develop a leadership program for undergraduate students. The alumnus, Mr. Smith, earned his MBA from XYZ University and is the president and CEO of a large tech startup firm. The president and vice president of university advancement have approached the Division of Student Affairs, specifically the Office of Student Leadership and Engagement and the College of Business, to inquire about collaborations to cultivate this donor and establish a gift. The president has charged your offices with identifying a focus for the award, including:

- What academic level (first year, second year, junior, or senior students) could be identified for the award?
- Is there a specific focus, such as women's leadership, an academic program, or collaboration between academic and student affairs programs to promote this award?

Your group has been asked to form a team of four individuals from the Office of Student Leadership and Engagement and the College of Business to develop a plan for the $100,000 recurring gift and to present this plan in five days to the vice president for university advancement, the president, and Mr. Smith. Here are some key questions for your team to consider:

1. What data does your group need to make a compelling case to Mr. Smith?
2. What data do your group have access to at the institutional, divisional, and college levels? If the data do not already exist, is there a way to obtain it quickly and responsibly with permission?
3. For collaboration, what do your units need to maintain in terms of services? Do priorities need to shift to "make room" for this donation? What specific agreements do the two entities need to reach to ensure a smooth collaboration?
4. How will the data, collaboration, and proposal be presented to the president, vice president of advancement, and Mr. Smith? What information would be the most effective in establishing a compelling case for support?

Appendix B

How Clemson University Reports Progress in Student Affairs Goal Areas

1. Clemson University Interactive Factbook: www.clemson.edu/institutional-effectiveness/oir/factbook/index.html
2. Clemson Elevate Dashboard: Elevate Dashboard | Clemson University https://www.clemson.edu/elevate/dashboard.html

About the Authors

Dr. Amber Fallucca serves as the inaugural director of the Carolina Experience at the University of South Carolina (USC), an office dedicated to a comprehensive undergraduate experience through an emphasis on transfer, sophomore, junior, and senior year students. Dr. Fallucca previously served as USC's Quality Enhancement Plan Director and Associate Director in the Center for Integrative and Experiential Learning. She also serves as Affiliate Faculty in the College of Education teaching courses in the Higher Education and Student Affairs program and in the South Carolina Honors College. Dr. Fallucca's scholarly and practitioner experiences focus on higher education assessment, design and accessibility to experiential learning and additional meaning beyond the classroom engagements, and experiences of student populations on the college campus.

Dr. Dena Kniess is an associate professor in the Department of Counseling, Family Therapy, and Higher Education at Appalachian State University. She received her Ph.D. in educational leadership - higher education from Clemson University, an M.A. degree in college student personnel from Slippery Rock University (Pennsylvania) and a B.S. in English-writing from Slippery Rock University. Dr. Kniess' research foci include assessment in higher education, college student access and success, faculty development, and multicultural issues in higher education.

About the Publisher

The National Resource Center for The First-Year Experience and Students in Transition was born out of the success of the University of South Carolina's much-honored University 101 course and a series of annual conferences focused on the freshman year experience. The momentum created by the educators attending these early conferences paved the way for the development of the National Resource Center, which was established at the University of South Carolina in 1986. As the National Resource Center broadened its focus to include other significant student transitions in higher education, it underwent several name changes, adopting the National Resource Center for The First-Year Experience and Students in Transition in 1998.

Today, the Center collaborates with its institutional partner, University 101 Programs, in pursuit of its mission to advance and support efforts to improve student learning and transitions into and through higher education. We achieve this mission by providing opportunities for the exchange of practical and scholarly information as well as the discussion of trends and issues in our field through convening conferences and other professional development events such as institutes, workshops, and online learning opportunities; publishing scholarly practice books, research reports, a peer-reviewed journal, electronic newsletters, and guides; generating, supporting, and disseminating research and scholarship; hosting visiting scholars; and maintaining several online channels for resource sharing and communication, including a dynamic website and social media outlets.

The National Resource Center serves as the trusted expert, internationally recognized leader, and clearinghouse for scholarship, policy, and best practices for all postsecondary student transitions.

Institutional Home

The National Resource Center is located at the University of South Carolina's (USC) flagship campus in Columbia. Chartered in 1801, USC Columbia's mission is twofold: to establish and maintain excellence in its student population, faculty, academic programs, living and learning environment, technological infrastructure, library resources, research and scholarship, public and private support and endowment; and to enhance the industrial, economic, and cultural potential of the state. USC is among the top universities receiving Research and Community Engagement designations from the Carnegie Foundation.

To learn more about the National Resource Center, visit www.sc.edu/fye. To learn more about the University of South Carolina, visit www.sc.edu.